Contents

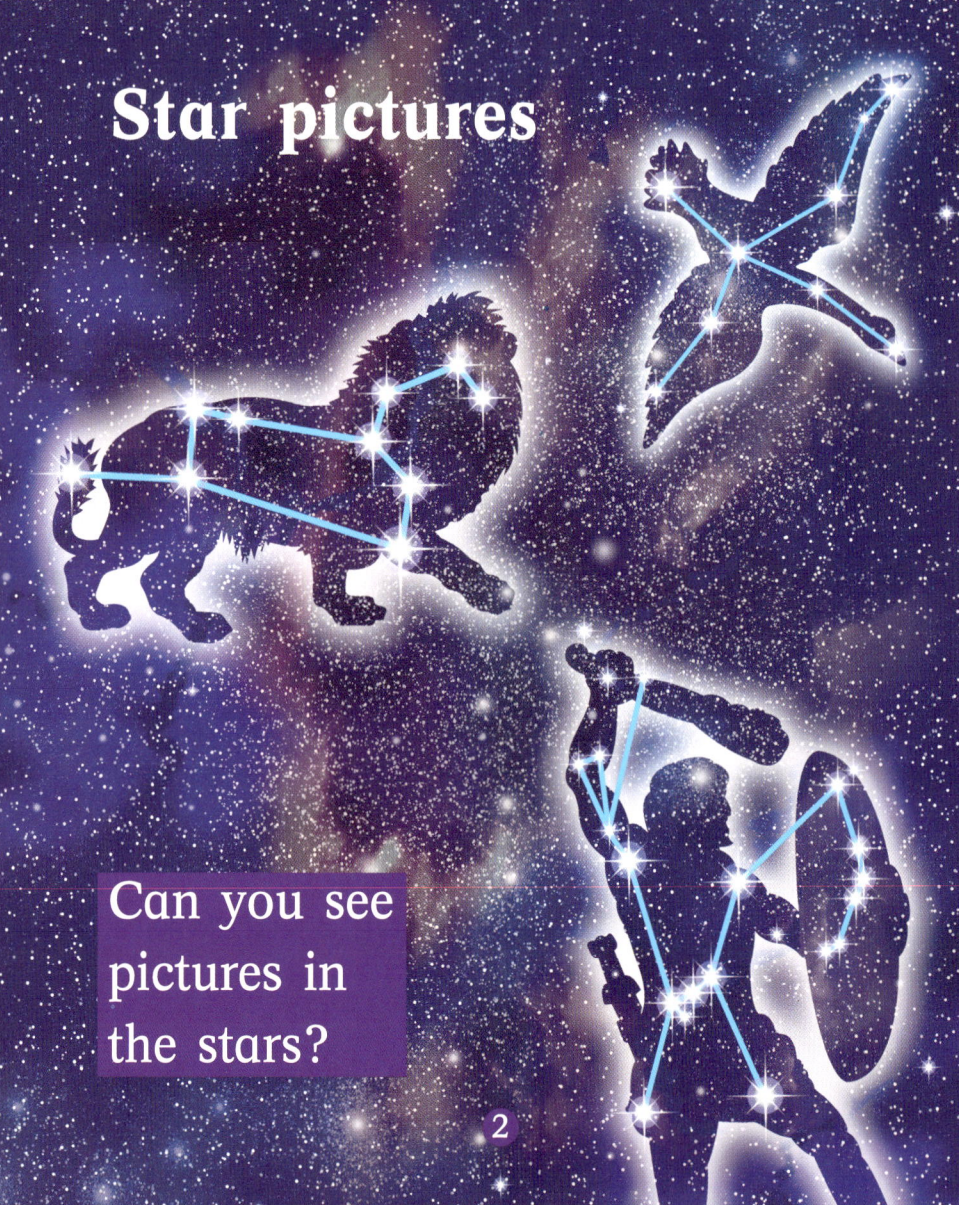

Star pictures

Can you see
pictures in
the stars?

2

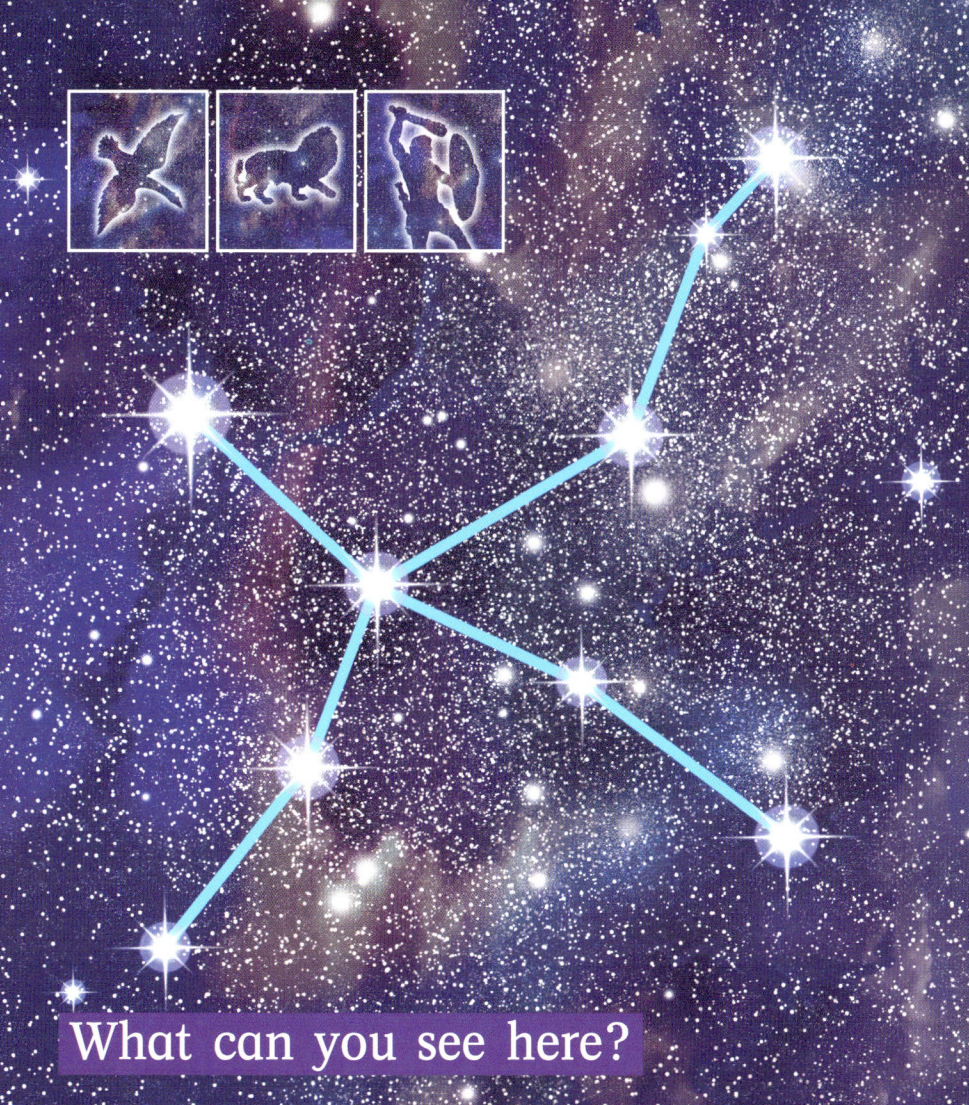

What can you see here?

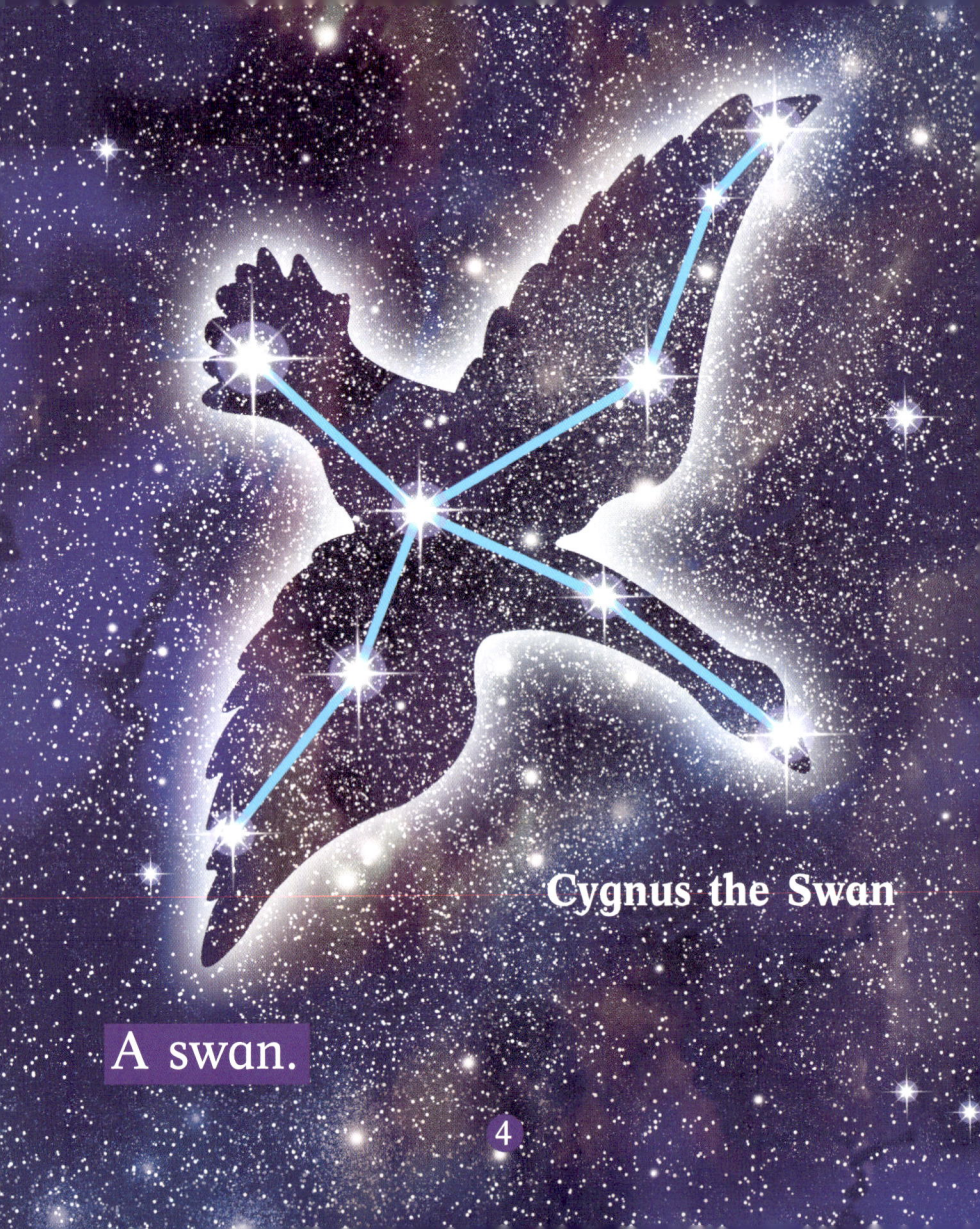

Cygnus the Swan

A swan.

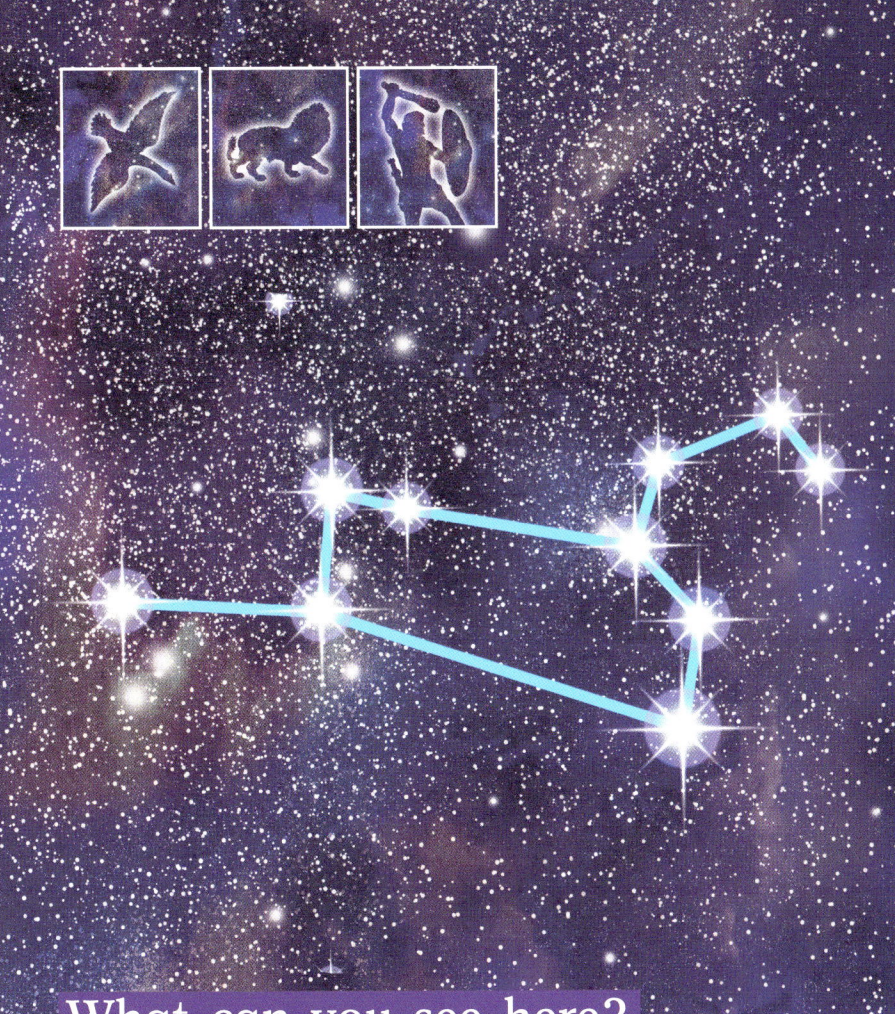

What can you see here?

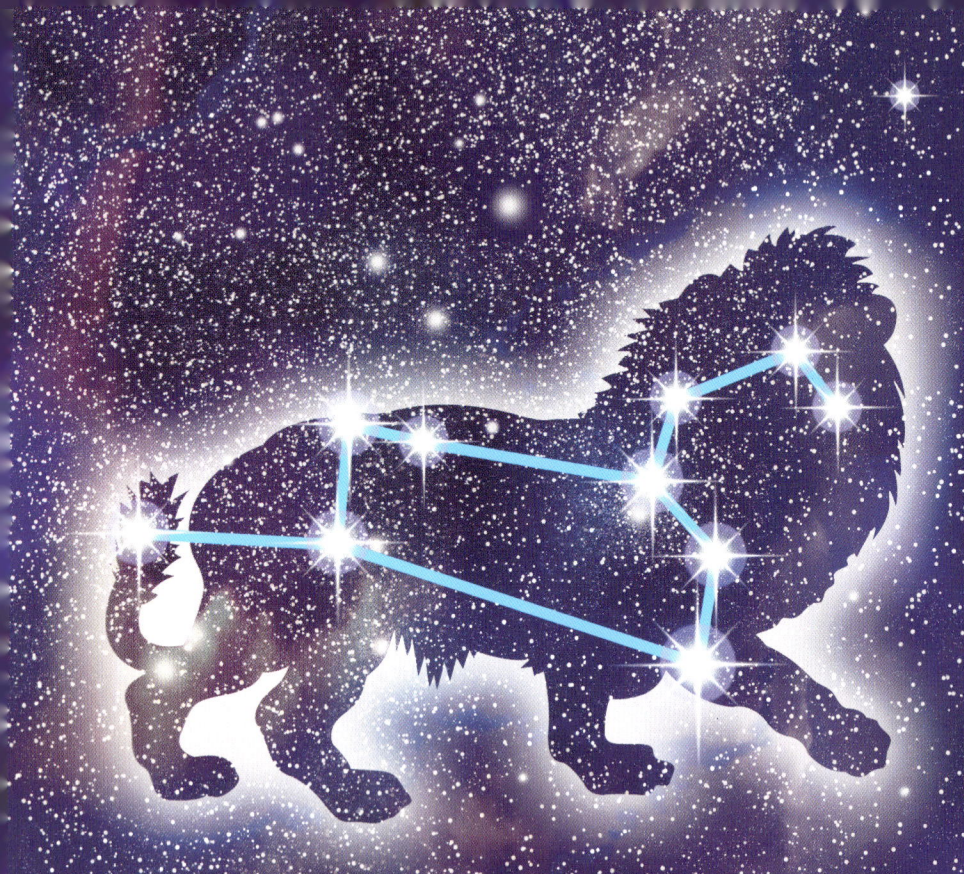

Leo the Lion

A lion.

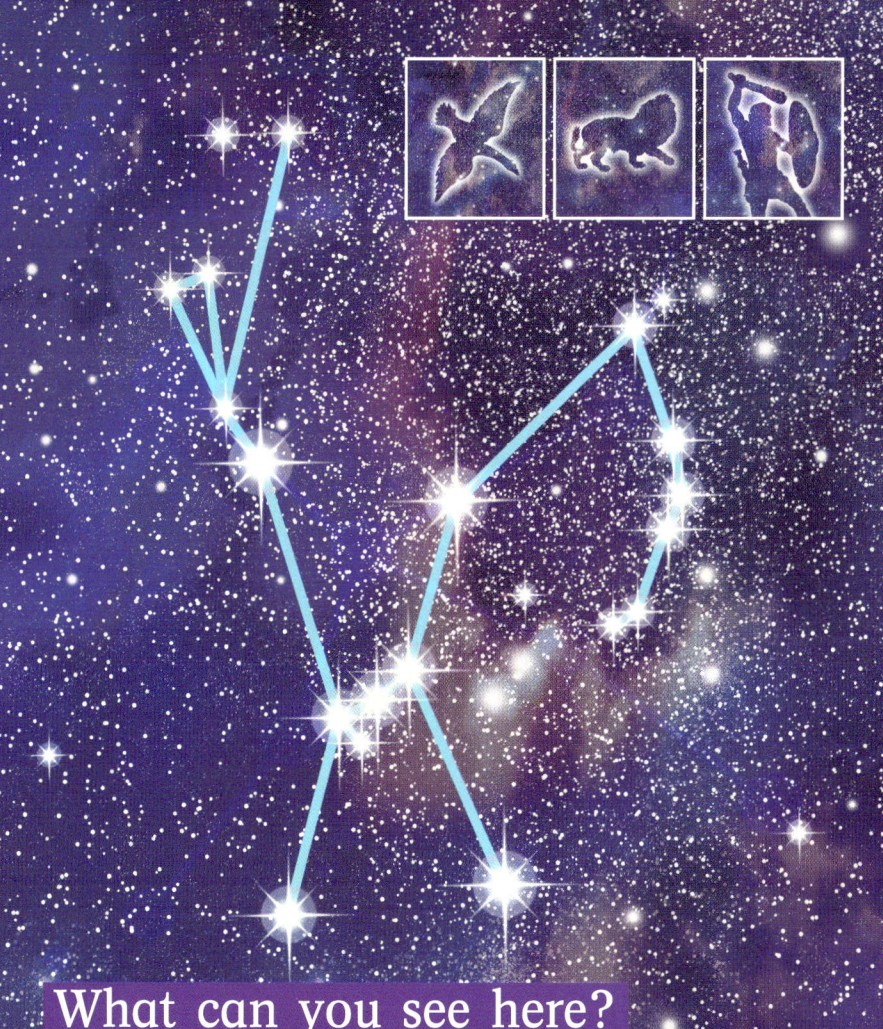

What can you see here?

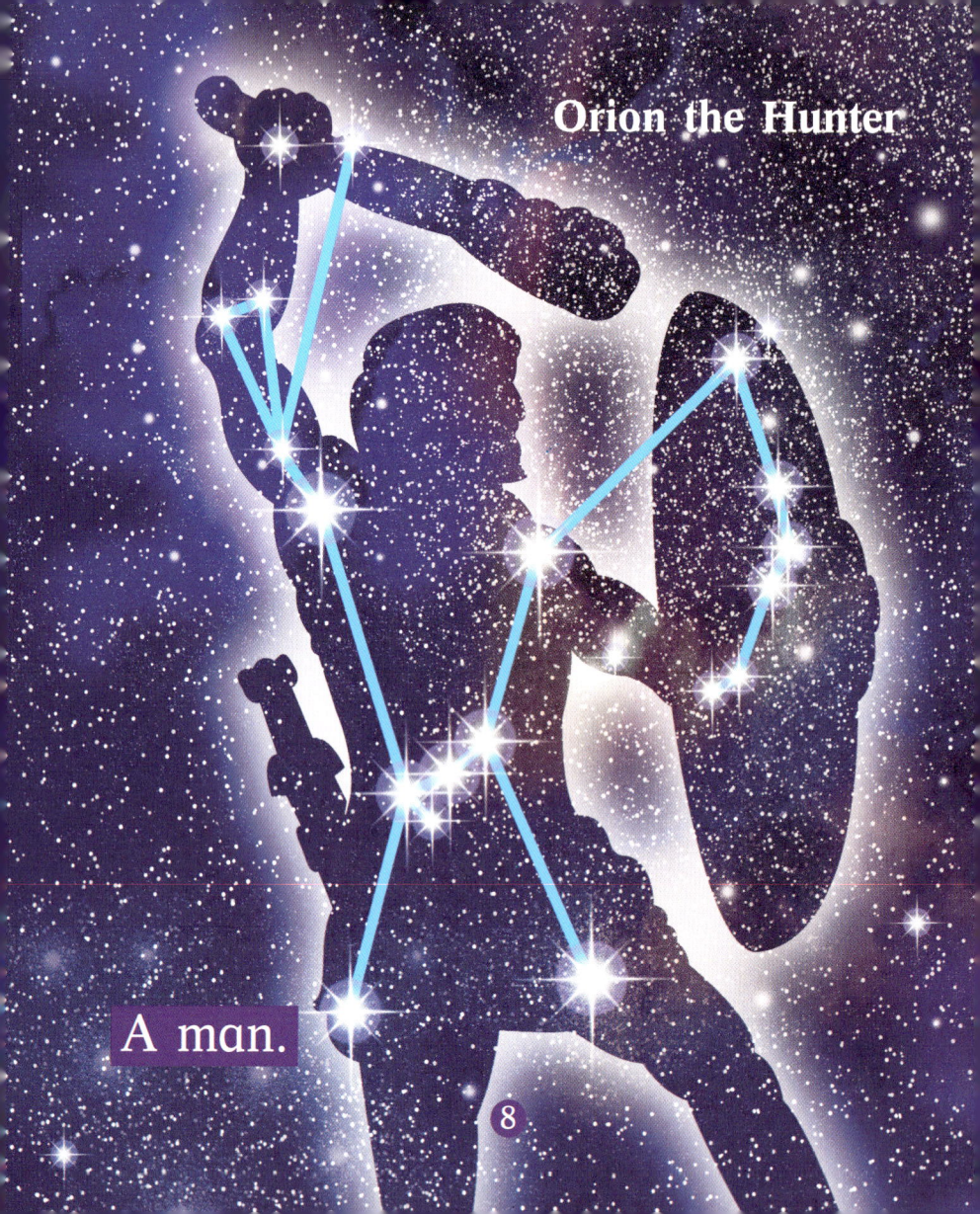

Orion the Hunter

A man.